I0111536

CONVERSATIONS WITH SKELETONS

BY

TRINOMIOUS ADONIS

Copyright © 2018 by Trinomious Adonis

All Rights Reserved.

No part of this book may be used or reproduced

in any manner whatsoever

without written permission of the

publisher, except where permitted by law.

ISBN-13: 978-0-578-45281-4

# TABLE OF CONTENTS

In room 742

For seven hundred and forty two days

I wanna to be your man and love you 742 ways

Using my brush to paint you abstractly

In purple and grey shades with...slight hints of

Yellows and reds to signify our bodies ablaze...cause

Together we radiate and tonight we'll glow and

In 742 seconds we goan glisten like

Two fleeing sweaty slaves cause

Together we're both hand in hand and

From the world we decided to escape

So now look at us...we're on a back woods mission

Creating unified trails towards ecstasy

That we both decided to pave

Riding this...majestic sonic wave onto

Symbolic roads of concurrence

The dreamy look in her eye the only reassurance needed

To confirm this evenings purpose

So please cum...employ my heart and

Till the end of our time I swear, I pledge, I promise

To search all of those zones encoded erogenous with

Nothing but alluring homogeneous movements

Simulating the stimulating rapturous

Emotions that run...wild like raging rivers

Flowing rapidly out of control

Down, down, down, that...flowing canyon of beloved gold

Shit...us being here alone on its own is a

Situation one could consider bold

Yet...here we are, feeding like savages on buried desires

Seven hundred and forty two hours old

Sipping on that...Jamaican rum

Pulling on that...homegrown

While I...cough and you choke

Shit a...hit for you, a sip for me the two main ingredients

Needed to help us relax and laugh

Before fate would have us

Take off one another's clothes

As our...tongues finally empathetically embraced

As we spiritually eloped...only moments after

I dropped to my knees to feast and

Meticulously all in between them

Butterscotch thighs like a hot press

That valley I combed

Giving explicit attention to

Every sexy mole, hole that cavern, that tavern

For...I am the match to your oil that lit

That spark and brought that flame back to your

Oh so fading lantern

I've been...waiting for this moment since 1995

So let's forget about tomorrow and

In unison engage in an untamed passion

As I...rise up from the depths

Dizzy from just bestowing upon you that

Vicious tongue lashing

Crashing any of your wildest preconceived

Notions and ideas of how I taste and if I'm

Really about that action

Look at you, laying there...hypnotized well under my spell

Basking in the joy of my erotic, eccentric covetousness

As I pull you to the edge of the bed and

Proceed to show you just how good my flex is

Whispering to you softly...look at me

As I apply long firm hits from my pelvis too your hips

Loving the feeling of me inside you

While you convulse with an

Uncontrolled sensual epileptic fit

Remembering the look on that face when

I fell into them two lips and told you

This feast is for you mama

This...gourmet platter of filet mignon dick

That keeps going and growing

Cause we...timeless is this session baby

This is our moment and tonight I promise

To be...nothing but infinite

I'm addicted to you baby

I'm like a...lush and his habit and

I'm starving for another hit as my mouth

Rages and massages those picturesque breasts

While we both...nearly drown

From all the sweat that falls down upon us

Like a Swiss mountain top avalanche

Down my head, down my neck onto your

Luscious Jell-O jiggling chest

As I softly nibble on your ear you

Lightly scratching upon my back while

Together we enjoy a symphony like no other that

Creates noisy collisions on not so innocent kitty cats

Sounding off for the neighbors

Smack...smack...as I continuously...smack...smack that ass

Searching for that universal moment of truth

That last incredible stroke of fate that

Melts my candle and causes me to feverishly

Run out of gas...our destiny arriving at

Avenue pleasure at last...born and unearthed just

Seven minutes and forty two seconds after

The clock struck twelve and the...previous day passed

Having me mark this day in our history

In our Love calendar as

The best first fuck I believe I ever had!

# A LOVE UNTITLED

I can't help missing you

It's just the kind of man that I am

I can't help wanting to kiss you

I just keep remembering the days gone by of

Holding your pretty face with the

Gentle touch of my docile yet

Desperate hands

I've been trying to let you go for so long but

After holding on for so long

There seems to be a part of me that's become

Too attached...I can't

I can't stop thinking about our...lost romance

I can't stop thinking about our...thing of the past

Ever since we've stopped I've starved

Its' been good Friday everyday look at me

I've thinned out from the fast...turbulent

Emotional roller coaster ride

A breathtaking journey experienced

From the front seat of a love Jones all

In-between the seam of your thighs

While It's you who had me

Lost at sea admiring precious smiles

Holding hands with God while lost in heavens eyes

Throughout the best and worst of times

All within the stint of a year I've learned the value of

Gains and losses because with you

I've lived a lifetime, and

Anything and anyone after you

Can in no way possibly compare

It's simply just a...waste of my plentiful time...

# AFTERSEXAFTERSHOX

It's been about one week and two days late and

Yet my earth still quakes and

Shatters upon the souls of my feet

I find myself confined to small spaces

Living out sad songs

Mesmerized by the pleasure while

Dually assaulted by the grief

I can't eat...haven't been able to sleep

I've been up nightly since seeing her last and

I'm about to break out in hives cause

I'm edgy...damn

What the fuck has she done to me?

She's got me all uptight and...out of sync and

I doubt she could even possibly understand

How or why I keep having these

Multiple infallible visions of chocolate wonder

Filling my hands and mental as I tell you

I believe it's her I see

Looking as beautiful as ever...simply e-x-t-r-a-ordinary

Staring softly into my eyes

As I...revel within this moment and

Replay that event like its stuck on a loop and

I'm trapped inside of a...lifetime exercise cause

It's two days later and I still find I'm

Acting out a scene from my very own

Requiem in delight and

I'm telling you the feeling couldn't be any more

Piercing...vivid...bright

Acoustic electric...front row

Purple Rain Tour live and it's...solely

I who can't wait to again take a running start

Jump and swan dive...deep into the abyss of those

Two luscious...precious...heart formed lips

This thought alone causes this man to

Stand alone staring off into the sunset...motionless

Envisioning the both of us

Laughing and dancing only moments before

Rolling and crashing upon the shores of

A...forever eternal bliss

Lost in a storm of rage and fury it's just she and I

Embarked and engaged in another long lasting

Passionate endearing enigmatic kiss

This here, this is the

Tale of the fantasy acting out on the wish...and

By all powers vested in me

By no means will it ever end

Because for her...I'm in a full blown lust and

My body I just wanna give lend and spend

Praying down on bended knee to heaven above

Her Love...she'll merely bless me

Again and again and again...and

On this dick do a little...stretch twist and bend

A little to the left...a little to the right...up and down

Side-to-side back to front over and over again and again

This time from the couch to the shower

To the bed, to the car, to the counter in the kitchen

Washer, dryer onto the lazy boy in the den!

Damn baby...what the fuck are you trying to do to me?

Got me dreaming about you

Blacking out and staggering from that

Overdose caused by my

Sweet tooth infatuation...cause

AfterSexAfterShox is the word of the century and

It's what I want you to be like me

To be simultaneously having

While you grab from the multitudes of

Metaphorical images of me

Out of the Earth's clear blue sky

Cause...on the topic of me

I want you to forever to remain

Black hole deep...astronomically high

Well...maybe not that deep but kinda like...as if

I were the clouds and you were the rain

Can you...feel the passion in my words?

Can you...envision the beauty of what I'm saying?

Because together on top of the world

With all this in mind

Could it be you and I as the proverbial

King and Queen where we could

Both be together and possibly forever

Perpetually reign?

# ASHIMIWI

Curious eyes aligned with

Timid smiles and bashful grins

That lie across tranquil faces

Is how it always begins

I...stare you stare

We...handshake

I ruminate "soft" damn

Little does she know that instantaneously

Energy has just been injected and immediately

The warmth systematically transcends

Subtly...from her soul to mine as

I feel her pleasures and she dually feels my pains

Till...volts shoot through my heart and

I count each chill that treks up my spine and I find

Myself becoming more and more inclined

To ask for that name

To...take that long lonely walk off in the distance

That...lonely walk of fame

Deep, deep, deep

Down into the valley of the shadow of death

As...Ashimiwi takes over and I close my eyelids and

Glide over every single syllable

Delivered from her heavenly pure

Delectable apple cinnamon breath

While various thoughts of

Streams, waterfalls, rivers, lakes

Oceans, condensation...rain

I...she...me...we

Together...sweating...wet

Become every forth-coming thoughtful event for

Multiple days to cum as...she reigns torrential

On my fertile, carnal, carnival and

I cum...ridiculously close

In fact...nose to nose with those distant remote

Revelations of rich radiant rainbows

Those...euphoric colorful escapades acted out

In the name of lust under various erotic episodes

Which...daily I struggle to camouflage

To my rapid fire heavy panting chest...so tell me

How shall I dare reveal my emotions and

Toss my cards on the table or

Do these feelings I hoard ignore and mask?

Simply releasing her hand and allowing her to just

23

Respectfully...pass me on by as I...ponder the self

Inflicted suffocation of my sprouting stimuli and

Consider the passing up of a possible

Romanticized silent stare at...point blank range

Face to face...eye to eye

Not accept this dance, resist temptation at its finest

While walking away from the slow dance of a lifetime

Envisioning pelvis to pelvis

My thigh in-between her thigh

My push to her pull, my grind to her grind all

Underneath the pale dim moon of my inner city

Galaxy of our fading neighborhood street lights

How far will it go...how long it will last?

This frivolous plight of self inflicted mental suicide

Hell...I don't know and at times I don't even care as

I struggle with the call and decide

Not to let go of her hand just so I can revel

Within this moment, open my arms and

Let this...lust take flight

Acquire them digits, call her up and

Rap on the phone till the forthcoming

Break of destiny's daunting daylight

Living for the now...my stolen moment

Selfishly to never be concerned

With the thought of anything past tense,

That would make since in

Retrospect or in...hindsight

Neither the cause nor the ripple effect that one day

Just might...reveal the unjust ways I chose

To live in this complicated life as

Tired I grow from always second guessing the motives

As I raise my fist in anger beckoning morality to fight

All of the vicious demons that haunt, conquer and

Ultimately with these thoughts...imprison my nights

Forcefully...against my will keeping me incarcerated

To suffocate slowly in silent small square spaces

Those...dark evil places where exiled arch angles

Purposely place the tasteless...tantalizing images of

Taunting tempting faces on extravagant provocative

Mock stages to pose for what seems as if ages and ages

As I ponder the purpose for the petitioning of

My...psychotic phobic psychosis

Which ultimately only in the end leaves me with the

Thought...who in God's name could had written this

Malicious manuscript this...detrimental mental

Masquerade that keeps me fading precariously into black

To be lost for days upon days until I become the

Soul keeper of my crypt equipped with only

Distant dreams of

I...She...Me...We

So, do I need her no but...I want her and

Without her...I am incomplete...un-hole...sick

A victim caught in a windmill of my own creation

Lost...within the thrill of the moment

As I remain hell bent on trying to shake it off

A...fruitless cold turkey attempt at

Trying my best to stop and quit so

Months pass, days pass, hours, minutes, seconds

But it never fails as...Ashimiwi always seems to

Comes back and...eventually I start to

Nod out...fiend and...get that itch

Hello my name is Ashimiwi and

I'm sorry to say this but

I am a habitual love addict!

# BROKEN SPELLS

A living hell

A once...lifetime contract

An under the table deal with the Devil

You see she...evil

With her medieval spells and witch Dr. tactics

For she...bore the mark of the beast

But I being naïve couldn't see

Taking hits of her daily not knowing that

I'm already an addict

So I drank her potions daily while hoping

I would never wake up to ultimately be saved

From...living in a state of catatonic

For I was her...love slave and

All of my feelings and emotions in a bottle she saved

All of my dreams and fantasies she pillaged, she raped

She had me defying the odds and

Abandoning all I believed to be true

For a world with...two moons and a reality staged

While pounds and pounds of unholy love we made

In lust...we faithfully bathed

Fluids...we graciously exchanged

Until one day everything changed

No more conversations, no more pet names and

 Somehow I stopped licking her dry and

Without a court order she ceased draining my vein

Fuck...somebody tell me

What in the hell part of the game is this?

What happen to it forever being mine and

All the rituals she created that always involved complex

Heavy breathing and all those feelings intense?

At first I couldn't take it and...emotionally I felt sick

I was heartbroken and all alone because

Her I actually thought I missed

Until time cured all my ills and I discovered that

Loneliness was the illness

The spell had been broken and

Eventually a light came on and

Just like Cinderella

She became just another plain ol' bitch!

# DENIAL

For one too many days and

One too many nights

My candle has remained lit for you

Glistening in my window pane like

My favorite star that hangs high

Above the evening clouds

Buried within the black sky

It burns every night

Hoping that one day

You'll catch its glimpse and simply

Come back to me, decide to stay awhile and

Forever share my life

But so far so sad

No luck at all as one year has gone by and

Still no dice

As time waits for no one

S-l-o-w-l-y rolling by

Meanwhile hollow bones grow

Weak from lack of you

Missing your touch

Your glow, your kiss, your warmth, your sight

Constantly asking myself the

Questions of which I'm already knowing

The answers as to why

This thought and it's weight

Somehow have become inconceivable

As I'm left trying to fool myself

Never wanting to believe that I was and still am

The sole cause of all my

Current troubled unhappy times

I guess it leads to one conclusion that

I am one among the living with vision yet...blind

I can't let you go

I refuse to let you out of my mind...and sadly

I believe I could sorrowfully end this way

Leaving a candle lit for you

Hoping that one day you'll come back

Hoping that one day I won't end

Going completely mad

Going completely...out of my mind...

# DESIRE

A crime of the world

So perfect it could never be

Yet so familiar is the feeling

That in my mind I find that

Criminal it could never be

The awakening...a harsh reality

Which causes me to...sit silently

Wishin that all the naysayers

Would just go away and let us be

So we can just...skate around this

World on wheels, hummin, holdin hands

Immersed within our own beat

LA confidential yea...and so what if we

Living within the delusion of a provisional destiny

But somehow it doesn't seem to bother us

As we're both well aware of

All the unfortunate inconsistencies

Yet it is we who still choose to

Weather this self induced storm

Brush all the hate from off our shoulders

Play it off and...act numb to the world as

We tongue kissin as the strobe lights burn bright

As fog lights while we slow winding

In the middle of the dance floor

Making us...no less responsible for

Any actions of which I already needed a bucket for

As my cup hath runneth over for my spill has

Gradually graduated from a leak

Into a rapid raging pour because

So greedy I became that I couldn't help

But take what's not mine and

Continuously still have the nerve

To ask for...more, more and more

So if you could...won't you please just

Do me a favor and commit to give me

More, more and more?

Promise you can handle all this love and

Anything else for you that I secretly have in store

Cause, for the record

I need to be certain, I gotta be sure

So I...pick her brain daily and

Ask her all the questions of which

She hates to open up to counter

The kind that pick the locks to sacred tombs

In secret valleys that I swore on my life

To make it an obligation to explore

In the late dark of night I...exhausted

Yet for her I trek ahead...for her I must endure

With eyes my favorite color she watches me as

I frame my essence around her body and

Nestle up to every crease and cozy up to her every contour

While I stick like honey to

Every curve, corner, edge...bend

Loving the look of blue lace

Laying high upon that thigh resting so appealing

Up against that pretty ass caramel skin

It's they, these...felonious thoughts

Assassinating my cerebral and any futile attempts

To preserve my life to get me up out of this

Immoral ocean of debauchery guilt and sin

We be...moving so fast that catastrophic

Can be the only appropriate end

While we...speed and swerve

Down this one-way highway

Dead into a lust to the point where I can't even

Enlighten the masses as to how it even all began

Was it a handshake a traditional embrace?

Shit, maybe I just showed up like a thief

In the night and with the right words

The right smile I...cracked that combination

That made her all mine and in the interim

Caused her to open her heart and

Allow me in to exercise that body and essence

Cause honestly

My dreams she's already infiltrated and

Her soul I've already respectfully

Packed up and moved in

So...believe me when I say that

Together forever we will always remain as one and

Without her...I seriously doubt that

I could ever move on and live

So please accept this as my solitary confession and

Allow our spirituality alone to define how we will

Universally stay cosmically connected to

Forever remain lovers and

Eternally the best of friends!

# FADED

The faded traces of

A profiles silhouette

Is the one artifact

That I desperately hold

Awhile...the many seasons have changed

Time has advanced

Time has...graciously taken Its toll

As each moment passes by

It's once lucid engraving

Has been damaged by the wrath of nature

One of those, great eastern blinding summer sand storms

Massive tornadoes commanding

Furious outcomes to a far, far-away

Cold western world...and as

Distant as a glorious Sun rise

Yet as close as those treacherous dreams

That I detest and loathe

All reoccurring nightmares

All describing in detail

How mi amour don't want my love anymore

Leaving me as blank as

A canvases potential and the

Promise to become a portrait of

Great possibilities that have not yet been born

The sentiment of a man

Hollow, shabby...torn...scorn from your needs

A suicide in its self as our

Affinity has deceased and now alone

The tears in my eyes imply how I grieve

For my hunger and fancy for you

Had rapidly turned into an obsession

As you became my lust

I was over taken by greed

You see, mentally I've...perished without you and

To get you back I'd bleed

Slice chunks out of my own flesh

In a selfish attempt

Just to prove to you my love

Just to show you about you yea

I might be a little crazy

But this is all your fault

This is how you made me

I was fine before I met you but

After you left, since then

You given me day mares and satanic night dreams

You've...laced my body with cold sweats

Struck me down like a sinner

With thunder bolts from the heavens above and

The roar of...hellish lightning

When all I ever wanted from you was for you to

Indenture my employment and

For you to just trust me and

Allow me to be your...erect pleasant and

Most affectionate slave

While...asking you with reverberation in my voice

Why won't me you just save?

Instead of leaving me riding the waves of

The cosmos on today's miserable falling star

Mother Earth

Sadly being lost I've stumbled

Sadly being lost I've searched...having searched

I've found while becoming astonished at the discovery

Because what I found was nothing near to being sound

For the thing that I had been searching for

At times left me by the clutches of

Misery...trapped, confined and dumfound

Listening close to my heart the feeling in

Repetition the words that resound

Louder and louder...in out...echoing around and round

Towards the direction that I pray

For at the foot at my imagination lives the

Idol I created in my mind

That I foolishly praised every day

This fine creature of nature

Sprawling within the light

Inside of a brilliant fireball that

Illuminates and glows till eternity

Keeping me warm...constantly soothing me right

To the point where I can rest easy and tell myself that

Not having you is not the worst thing in the world...but

It's ok and eventually I'll be alright...

# FLASHBACKS

Flashbacks

Relax and welcome the comeback

She and I alone French kissin' down low

Sunken in the luv seat of life

Trapped inside her cozy little...love shack as

Flashbacks

Talked to me and told me to take it easy

Slow it down and let this episode protract

So we can...kick back with soft music, dim lights

Slippery jelly's, ice cubes and Jim hats cause

Flashbacks

Pump life...I'm alive, extant

Lost in my own little world I'm a...buzzed insomniac

So...arraign my soul and arrest my cardiac

Cause believe me when I tell you that my lust is heavy

When all I can see are cloudy, steamy

Flashbacks

Of...she and I lost on various

Crusades with no...back pack unchained

We both tied up in love knots

Excited...cause no two positions were the same as

We...trekked all over the bed we

Sexed...deranged like wild beasts, estranged

Becoming the reality of two nymphomaniacs

Clearly out of our wits we both

Clearly clinically insane while

Emotionally I'm loving this game of

Her cat in my mouth while

I North and she South as

I Conquered that bed it's mine when

I was behind that bush in her house unmasked as

Flashbacks

Had us both out of control and...hunchbacked

As I ransacked her little love shack and

Hand delivered the warm milk

To feed her beloved little Kitty Kat and

With precise conviction I methodically

Launched my sneak attack as she would

Religiously follow the rules of

Sun Tzu and militarily counteract

Leaving me with these dark images to embrace

Which were those faded black and white Kodak's

Deep inside my psyche that I preserved like hieroglyphics

Telling vivid stories of a young Pharaoh's cherished

Flashbacks

Where...once upon a time

Shadowed movements proved to be as free and fluid as

Scriptures describing earlobes as the playgrounds

I used for the nibbling and the chewin

While the lips I delicately slid across

Played the apparatus for auspicious croonin while

We lay sideways...vertical...horizontal

Spoonin...screwin...doin...the hot damn muthafuckin nasty!

Causing these...penetrating earth shattering

Dazing, dazzling, deep demented impacts

Which led me to search for lost needles amongst

Mystical cyclical haystacks...all these

Detrimental essential

Flashbacks

Of foggy visions that traveled warp speed and

Brought me back to those times of old when

I systematically extracted all that

Apricot flavored climax...while setting fire to caramel thighs

I became that...passionate consummate pyromaniac

Who saw the fire he placed into her eyes

Whenever we heard the call of our wild

Where we'd always find time to

Somehow meet in the middle and allow our

Bodies to attach, engage and take flight

Hypnotic the only way I can explain how she's

Taken siege of my heart and moment by moment

Intricately began maliciously dirtying up my life

Because believe me when I tell you that when

My face and lips became the implant she needed as

She smashed it against her...mouth-watering

Everlastingly, forever February

Leaving me with this only question of

Flashbacks

How shall I...ever repay thee?

Where is the relational rumination

Where I rise up from the depths of

My own personal premonitions

Wiping my mouth caught out of breath

Within the axis of my own beautiful misery

Assessing this...post visual simulation in

Stimulation rapt in retrospection

Birthing the outcome...birthing the conclusion that damn

Her body and not the rum had to be the main concoction

The sole cause the...sole cold reason that

I came back for fourth, thirds, seconds

Blatantly committing all these harsh

Felonious acts of treason...and for what?

All for the purpose of

Me needing and wanting it so much

That I became a kleptomaniac and

Habitually stole for her love?

I mean a...moment here a moment there

A smooth criminal always on the run

Customarily fleeing the scene of the crime with a bag

Full of her fears, tears and a sack full of her emotions

When the only thing from our inauguration

She honestly offered me was

A pocket full of her time

How could I not take more than what was given

By season two and episode five?

When she confessed to me with buoyancy that

It was, is and forever shall continue to be all mine

My pussy curves to the shape of your dick!

Damn...how could I ever forget that line?

This is why I will never forget

This is why I eternally remain wrapped around her finger

Forever wrapped so tight

In a misguided imprecise late night

Flashback of you so

Thank you...thank you for staying within my mental and

Continuously giving back to me night after night

Our...beloved moment in...TIME!

# FOR THE LOVE OF YOU

I love her

Like nothin on this earth and

I want her

Do whatever it takes and

All I need is 5 minutes

Just to show her

That she can...count on me like time

Cause for her...I am the Mayan calendar and

I'd gladly use up my

13 waves of my evolution shit

I'm willing to go...spiritually broke for her and

Worship...shit...that's an understatement

I'm a sinner, I idolize and I pray to her

For I...Hail my Mary she's so full of grace

What I gotta do to implant my babies?

What I gotta do to get her to finally embrace

My...illicit transgressions those

Frontal...lobe transmissions?

Will she...gracefully conceive

My...telepathic injections as I

Attempt to infect her mind like she's

Already infected day to day disposition?

What else could it be but these

Bacterial Love blessings?

I'm sorry baby but...there ain't no cure for this and

All those...cold sweats you have at night that cause those

Sweet sticky clear...scandalous vaginal secretions

Leavin um dazed and confused

Yeah...at times that's how I've been known to leave um

But for her I'm constantly high and

Nightly she leaves me having hallucinations

Imagining for me she's reaching

To cure these ills and all my miniscule trials and tribulations

With...long deep kisses and...thrusts of hard dick cause

My semen holds the medicine

My...God If she only knew of these emotions

She stirs whenever I'm...standing in her presence

Whishing she would just choose me and believe in me and

Every day could be her birthday and

Every night she can claim her present

I touch she touch

I taste she taste

I caress she bends

I suck, lick, slurp...stretch it out

Set a course, GPS is on

Heaven has got to be the destination

As we...levitate off into the late of night and

Blast off towards the Milky Way

5, 4, 3, 2, 1...ignition

We've got lift off baby and we on the way to

Libra, Virgo, Sagittarius, Cancer, Pisces...Capricorn

Next stop...Sirius...on the way to Orion

Riding the cosmic waves of this

Love affair on the rugged back of Leo the Lion

From...the stars high up in the heavens

On down to the Sphinx and...Pyramids of Giza onto

The majestic peak of...holy Mt. Zion...

# FUTILE FRIVOLOUS FANTASIES

Forcefully succumbed

By the deliberate forces of nature

I lie...quiet...motionless...still

Dormant while sunken and soaked

Within my deepest

Darkest depressive lonely dimensions

I find myself thinking of you

Wanting to be with you

Hating myself for dreaming of you

Mad at the situation daily

Wanting to distance myself

From any and all thoughts of you

You see it's...all because of you that

This curse lingers and continues to brew

Long after the fire has died

Trapped inside are all the images and

Signs implying sequentially the reasons why

You still rule and...govern my life

Even after all this time

Several months and still counting

You remain the factor

That gleaming beacon of sorrow

That torments me endlessly

Relentlessly even after our demise

Damn...how do I rid my mind of those

Fucking penetrating eyes?

How do I run so far and fast that it transcends me

Into another way of living without

Remembering only forgetting our...moment in life

While...dually forfeiting and surrendering all of our

Instants in the spotlight and

All the brief blithe fragments of

Experienced blinded bliss...fuck it

I would give it all back to you if I could

Gift-wrap all this emotion up and special deliver

Back to you...return receipt requested

Every suspect laugh, hug and kiss

Every...promise, dream and wish

For every time you said you loved me

When all the bottles popped while

Scented candles blazed as our bodies

Ignited, radiated and lit the...final stage of

Our weathered, bewildered, premature biography

All before you...single handedly called it quits

All this...without even...telling me why or

Even kindly saying goodbye

Pathological unfaithful indiscretion

One should be more sensitive to

The feelings, the thoughts and the lives

That...one willingly reaches out to touch for

Futile frivolous fantasies sourly remind me

That on the scales of life

Pain always outweighs the joy...and

For the cost of love I emotionally

Paid and paid...to often...much too much.

# GIVE ME THAT

Sometimes I just cant

Help the way that I feel for you and I

Lose control

I let my thoughts consume the

Multitudes of sensations

Across every inch of my lonely body

Until the day you return

Until the moment it's you I hold

I need it and I want it and

There's no other way to

Explain the dialog in the script

To the story that is us and our

Critically acclaimed, world renowned

Broadway show...you see it's you

You've...lifted the curse you've broken the mold

So I...let down my resistance and in turn

Exposed my soul and ever since then a

Lustful love has been born and it

Keeps me wanting and waiting for what's

Right there, right in your

Little honey pot of gold

So to the future of us I say...let us toast and

Allow our bodies to radiate, glow and dance

Remember this is a celebration

Not take us for granted

While not letting any one thing

Come between us opportunity and...circumstance

I need to show you the blueprints

To my immaculate plans that

Summons and command

You to join me a mile high in the sky while

I ride and my body you frantically steer cause

There's nothing in the way stopping us

As all toll roads are open

All lanes are...wide, free and clear as

We're both in the fast lane of a lust

So baby buckle up as I prepare to

Downshift that body from 6th to 5th and

Right on down to 4th gear cause

I come to you naked with arms wide open as

My only intent is unadulterated honesty and

The juicy fruit that bare

Intentions symbolizing the sacred, angelic, holy, pure

Hot boiled exotic, erotic, erupting, exploding emotions

Over flowing for the sole cause of...your love

So come to me I beg of you

Walk out of my dreams, become my reality and

Let my hands explore that valley

While I slowly massage and rub that

Sweet, sexy, supple, honeysuckle

Caramel brown skin...imagine

Together we could melt like ice cream baby and

I'll be the butterscotch while you'll be the chocolate chip

That drips down nipples I've never known

To be so solid, erect, intense...just look at us

Off in a secluded room playing with one another

After all the scented candles were lit

As I submit my final request that you allow my

Hands and lips to be your breasts two new best friends as

I promise to rub & kiss each one of them both equally and gently

Making sure to not deny

Either one of them while my...hand ill send

Gliding around your corner, hugging every curve of

That...exquisite river bend

Gently making my way on down, down, down to your

Ramped raging white water canal

That...sacred place that's more sought after than any

Jewel that could lie face down

At the bottom of Africa's beautiful Egyptian Nile

As I...sail your seven seas forever and a day

Remaining content at being lost and never to be found

You see...It's you, you're...killin me softly with those

Avid moans...damn baby

I love it when you make those sounds

You know those...profound sounds that drown

Me in your arms then command me

To rise up from the ashes of your wrath caused by

Your...midnight summer solstice

Perilous southern storm to...delicately perform

Various warm...oral transactions that

When applied correctly exhume what

Dreams are made of them...iced out coffee n creamy

Habitual sporadic manic reactions such as

Sharp shrieks, deep gasps and heavy pants

That all add up to long red welt like tracks

That...hang like murals from sensual scratches on backs

Almost giving you that...dear thing you've been missing but

Somehow I maintain and reluctantly I hold back

Pausing only briefly in-between two beats of a

Passionate duplicate love sick heart attack because

I know where it's at and I know precisely how to give you

Exactly what it is you lack as I...rise to the occasion of

Lifting, spreading legs then sliding on in

Licking your fingers as a sign

My green light to softly commence

The...skill of a seasoned warrior...as I

Gently begin tapping on skins

While...nostalgic tones of war chants

Govern you to rhythmically and

Repeatedly to...sing to my hems by

Way of...seismic percussion's in intimate

Imminent candle lit discussions while

Bass strings pop and

I feel like the king of your soul and not pop

Mastering your song in the key to your life

Cause you're my...pastime paradise as

I rock the Wonder of Stevie conquering you all fucking night

Maliciously feeling my way around while blindly pulling hair

Wickedly and wildly as we fuss, cuss and fight

All in-between the...licks kisses and bites as I

Stare into your ebony eyes and

Chase you up the walls you playfully climb

Then...back down again except this time double time

Freefalling from the various enchanted

Thoughts of her in my mind combined with

Our sweat and shine

We make...puddles of lust that splash from

Illustrious strokes whenever her I'm...deep inside

That...grand piano playing my love concerto

Making sure to never miss a note on her...ebony and ivory keys

As this is...verse two and section three of

My love serenade the part where I aggressively

Reach for that climax and

Smash her lovely tambourine

Extracting all those joyous fruitful flavors of passion

Which makes me love the idea of backstroking

In the warm water lakes of her

Tasty mango cream till

Dreams of me forever bathing under that waterfall

Infiltrate my mental and my candle melts feverishly

As we...empathetically yell, holler and convulse

Through...cold chills and together let out

A...passionate, orgasmic, tantric, silent scream

While...my babies are all off on a brand new journey

In formation

Butterfly stroking intensely

Up your

Majestic candied stream!

# HOLDING ON

They remain one with me

These...thoughts of this reoccurring dream

One of the ones that never seem to go away

Only leaving and coming back

Leaving and coming back, returning every night

While I'm offline mentally, visiting

Enchanted lands where pretty faces dance

Upon pillow clouds as exotic birds

Drenched of melancholy sing

Downtown Detroit blues...simply because its surreal

A wish of all things believed to be feasible that

In time...reveal themselves as untrue

While empathy fills up and eventually overflows

Subtle hallow ducts of evaporated emotions

Inspiring these...telepathic sensations

To travel from your soul directly to mine

All relevant...all in time

Meanwhile, in the back of my mind

I remind myself of a not so far off place in time

When...distant gazes were stir fried and shaken

With...elevated fantasies and praises that

Couldn't help but plague this man's most

Undeserving lonely existence as it...left me

Caught up in-between a three staged reality of

What I perceived to be the right and wrongs of

Losing out on the lessons of lust for an

Unrealistic love affair within a...troublesome

Confusing life continuation...the conundrum

Left me sitting alone sulking, choking

Amongst a polluted breeze stuck on

The swings of contemplations moral pendulum

At least in the interim as I

Had to imagine harder and harder

Somehow picture it all in High Definition

Two majestic hues that glow, spread, comingle and blend

Into a...full bloom in union with

Shades that copulate to impregnate

Somehow...making a way for

Verbal tones of conniving accents

To be lost in rhyme...laid out as these

Descriptive quixotic intriguing phrases

Picking mental locks to

Free fatigued brains imprisoned by

Titanium self-made solitary confined cages

Neglecting the idea of attempting to fathom

The experience of being suffocated by a

Woman's warm and tender...lustful embraces as I

Daydream of tasting this tangy thought of the

Simplest loving touch-touch

While...baby hair tingles as a cheek and cheek

Pass full lips doused with

Flavorful scents while flawless

Skin on youthful faces brush...that moment when

Four arms, two hips and supple breasts press up against

A solid chest...all the while two

Seasoned yet soft hands remain

Laying at ease securely against

A quarter moon and its luminescent crescent

The feeling of grandeur that hypnotizes and concurrently

Gives birth to a love that maliciously slays the stress

Pleasure at nothing but its best

In full marriage within this quest

To hold the thought of her as

Close to my body as close can get

From day one to day out to sunrise to sunset

Onto whenever God decides to vengefully

Blow out these lights of a

Glowing hue so purposely iridescent

This...moment is when the both of us imagine

We could...finally be together for forever's

Eternal dawn to dusk

For whenever I close my eyes and visualize

This sequence I use my third eye

To see all the hot spots that you and I will

Emphatically touch as...I ask of you gently

Do you like?

As I whisper to you softly...don't blush

Merely just collapse in my arms and

Experience the wrath of this passion and

Deliberately French kiss

The musk scent of want that escapes my natural essence

Worship...the punishment handed down

All because your presence

Routinely commits these felonious crimes as

Your affection habitually steals my attention

While...not to mention my aching heart

This could be that one thing

That something, that initial start like

The instant a child is born and inherently

Begins to cough, breathe, see

Its unexplainable how all this is happening

You not knowing what's going on and

How I look at you like I'm a scoundrel, I'm the fiend and

How...deviously you've become

More than any simple want in my life

More than a simple voyage, more than a mission

A necessity in my life as the air that

Serenely surrounds my world

Somehow you've become my need!

# LOVE ON LIFE SUPPORT

Critical...the condition of this heart

Fragile is the situation

Because it feels as though

Through the passing of time I've lost you

Electricity...gone

The connection...broken

We be...missing the spark

So I...try not to let it weigh me down as

I hold my head high and

On the pain try not to harp

While I wear a disguise like Kent Clark cause

She be Superman's kryptonite and

I can only wonder why we even chose to start

Being the master archer that she is

It only made since that one day she would eventually

Shoot that arrow right through my heart

Bulls eye...right on the mark

As I forever bear the scar

A battle wound of pride that mark and

All the pain that goes along with it

So while I willingly rewind and

Press play to watch all the snippets

Fuck you...I love you

Calm breeze on the beach

Slowly...I'm touching you

City view from the hotel room

Repeatedly...I'm making love to you

Round one, two, three

Well actually round three I was fucking you

Cause...we were made for one another and

I knew your body like I studied it in school

But the only really bad part about it all is that

You ended up wanting too much

In fact...more than I could ever possibly give you

So why you fucking up the rhythm?

Why you fucking up the love?

Why you fucking up us?

Damn sweetie...shame on you!

# MOURNING AFTER

Sadness is the madness

Ever made love with a Devil in a red dress?

Become too attached then wonder why

It's always hotter than hell

Trying to coexist in relationship can never be blessed?

A heart can become a black hole...an empty mess

So I started a fire attempting to reach out by

Fanning my distress

Only to find out that she put us on hold...indefinitely

Immediately the relationship was in retrogress

And till this day...for her I swear I

Can't figure out why I'm so passionate

Meanwhile the scenario

Nothing short of classic...she push I pull

The surgeon of self inflicting pain

I think she's a...borderline masochist

The sole creator of our time and distance

A...mathematician in the making

The relationship author of

Dating while in Realm of Quantum Physics

The one with...all the answers who

Dreams in complex sequences

But can't see the sequence of events that led to us

Not being able to vocalize our apparent differences

While...all I be doing is dreaming about Shorty

My storm in a coke bottle...my darling little tempest as

Emotions stay stuck in a loop on replay

Reliving all those detrimental final kisses

Hanging over me like negatives in a dark room

Amongst the pain of her...miscued reverie

What shall be left of the fiber of he

If there can no longer be we?

I'd understand the future if I understood her past

But honestly...her life to me

Just happens to be a total mystery

Judge not, lest ye be judged

Words from many moons ago that at one point

She mistakenly volunteered to me

Giving me a glimpse of what was lurking inside

My God...how she so intrigued my curiosity

She became a personal conquest of which

I secretly idolized and prayed to annually

All in vain I suppose because even after all that shit

It still couldn't keep her next to me

So what to do now with all this empty space

This now...hollow shell of me?

Retreat, fall back and accept defeat?

Agree that I can't win um all so

I'll attempt to build Trump's wall

In a final attempt to keep her out of my mind emotionally

Not respond to her messages after

One quarter of being an absentee

Until I could really feel her reaching....and

I finally said fuck it and responded

Enjoy life and my number hey....just delete!

Fuck...did I just hit send?

Shit...can't hit message recall

Damn this Tequila really done got the best of me

Wearing my heart on my shoulder and

Attempting to stand on pride but fuck

Now I wanna tell her I didn't really mean it

Don't go...

How do I dare fix my mouth to tell her

I'm sorry?

# PASSIONATE

What the fuck?

Yeah, sometimes times

I have to ask myself

On the topic of us

Why the fuck is it...I seem to care so much?

I feel like I got here all alone with no help

From those customarily accused you know

Those...usual suspects

I thought we built this house together?

But you run whenever it's time

To get dirty and help clean up this mess

Emotionless...about as often as the

Ignorant card that gets played at leisure by

Thinking we playing checkers

When we been playing chess

Meanwhile...no regard for

This man's consciousness

Got me out here feeling a certain type of way

Thinking I can't be nothing else except

A skeptic on the topic of us and

It's making me feel like you

I can't help but second guess

So I...scribble down messages and

Dedicate poems that you don't even know exist

Depressing this love suicide

How many more times do you feel the need to

Sabotage my interest?

How many times do we have to call on EMS?

How many more resuscitations do you think I

Could possibly add to this failed life line before I

Throw in the towel cut all ties and

Eventually call it quits on us?

Decisions, decisions

Seems like lately you been making plenty for yourself

So in turn I think it's time for me

To do what I think is best

After all those years I invested in all of that round ass and

After all that sex...shameful

Waiting for you to have those two kids

Get married, get divorced

To only come to the conclusion that

I think I gotta say it was nice knowing you so

Good luck without me...God bless!

# PHEROMONES

Like a gentle breeze

She rapidly

Suffocated all of me

As I inhaled all of she

Exotic and sweet

Her...pheromones

Sticky

Inflicting fantasies of

Erotic pleasantries

Played out on

A deserted beach with

Palm trees and calm waves as

A heavy sun was setting

The mystique

Overflowing of intrigue

Fulfilling desires buried deep of a

Clandestine love affair

She's...infected me slowly and

Now I can't get

Her out of my head

I...can't get her out of

My...benevolent cross hairs.

# PITCH BLACK

Lights out

Fade my...heart to dark

Someone...blew out my eternal flame

Poured...Holy water on my illustrious spark and

Now I'm back where I came from

Back...staring at the mark

Wondering why it all began in the first place

Questioning the reasoning

Behind jumping the gun and

Committing this...false start

When all it ever was going to do was

Abruptly stop...dead in its tracks

Despite all the emotion endured and regardless of

How much I rapidly opened up and

How unexpectedly I became so affectionately attached

You see...somewhere along the line I got lost and

From reality I eventually became detached

I got caught up in her toxic chemistry and

Lost sight of all the facts and

Now I live a life in hell

Because with just one brisk stroke

She painted my entire world black

She...cold heartedly

Assassinated my love

A hit on a public street in broad daylight...damn

I had no idea how cold the bitch was

She...put me out of my misery leaving

Me alone in the darkness without question and

Without reason and allegedly just because

She claimed she was...falling in love?

So without just cause

She just...re-wrote the unwritten laws of nature

Becoming my executioner, jury and judge

She had no definitive authorization to do so

So what gave her the right abruptly kill my buzz and

Abandon the birth of our...unified emotion?

What type of strength must a woman possess to

Initiate this cause and effect and in turn like a light switch

Just...spontaneously disrupt

The eternal code of devotion and

Systematically issue some foreign

Uncontrolled, misconstrued interruption of

Cosmic, sonic, bionic energy which...ultimately

In the beginning had me with her fulfilling and

Has since left me without her...feeling empty

I...want her back but I won't ask

To beg for a love to return that should've have never left

In the first place...just simply isn't in me!

# SLIP INTO THE DARKNESS

It's electric

The energy that softly pulls you down to me

Descending blindly

Into the depths of a foreign obscurity

Which happens to be my own personal...security blanket

Which is...older than ancient Egyptians and

As obvious as my skin resembling

Ancient Egyptian inscriptions

Gifting...intricate descriptions

Using elaborate depictions of a wisdoms purity

All truth in, knowledge and understanding

Adding up to an air of

Superiority flowing within the mind

So slip into the darkness of my anima and

Watch the stars shine

A place with no borders...no boundaries

Only infinite...limitless time

That seem to wait for no one under the Sun

So pack your bags run and...come on and

Ride the train to destination destiny

Resting in the...company of a lavish sensitivity

While...applying massage therapy

To the psyche of your

Subconscious state of substance cause

For once it...seems in my life

I believe I've found something that I cannot live without

For your presence fills my emotional reservoir

Which causes tender feelings and wants

To burst mental levee's that

Nourish the brain and permit probing emotions to

Grow and sprout...crazy like wild flowers

So come find love in the open arms of darkness and

Become my wild fire...and as one, parallel to the Sun

We can burn the night away

In the glory of the midnight oil

Slithering in everything beautiful blackness

Holds close, owns and controls

You, me, the young, the old, the future, the past

The fathomed and unknown for

Mystique mystery and secrecy all surround

The splendor of halo within Cimmerian homes that

House inside of my head that I can't help but roam

For I am the spirit that dances to

Ancestral, tambour, tribal tones

All in the honor of your name

I sway...swirl...I hop and skip to put a spell on you

That summons you to my domain...by way of

Mental extrasensory proficiencies

A gift of god that was given to me

Something passed on by preceding generations of

Extraterrestrial extensions of family

So...by all powers vested in me...I bid to thee

Slip into the darkness and become my Goddess

I don't know what it is but I hold this

Farsightedness of the future and it's you and I that I see

Together as one reining on the

Throne of eternity continuously

Cruising on prolific journeys flourishing on enduring

Mental states of...ecstatic sanctity

So create in your mind beauty and

Consider blissfulness and

Dream of you and me!

# SLOWLY I RISE

Just the mere thought of you and

Baby slowly I rise

Slowly...I rise

You've allowed my

Dreams of you to become a reality

Whenever I stood upon your

Every wish, folded my arms and off

Majestic Thai cliffs into your Love

Backwards I...swan dived

Right Into your arms, lips and

All up in-between them

Heavenly chocolate thighs

Splash...

I am invading your world

The same way you have

Invaded my mind

Look at me

A creature so enthralled

Within your world

Your touch, your sound , your sight

All these...senses that

Became so, so, so alive

So...lets light this candle every night by our

Bedside and make slow, slow sticky love

No wait...scratch that

Let's aggressively fuck

To the flicker of the flame

While it burns and dances with us

Against the shadows of our bodies

Plastered against the adjacent walls

All

Damn

Night...

# SO GOOD

The pleasure extreme

Internally I explode

Mentally I self-destruct and holistically

I burst at the seams

For the attraction to she is

Too deep, she's...super supreme

Chemical in nature our

Bond our link and it's...curious how

Somehow I depict her as an extension of my

Emancipated psyche, bodily as if

She's actually holistically a part of me

A spiritual kind of yearning

She's...physically empowering

The remnants of several colorful images towering

That lie entrapped leaving behind

The scattered fractured fragrance of a

Perpetual metaphysical bliss

So strong, so placid, so meaningful

That...last detrimental femme fatal kiss

Albeit...born in the night it gradually

Delivers me directly into light

To the heights of an

Eternal maternal abyss

Where ancient ancestors

Congregate and uneasily rest

Knowing I'm not even supposed to be there then

Recklessly teleport me back to thee

Three dimensional equilibrial zones of Africa home

That...birth place of emotion that sewed the sentiments of

Tranquility while dually pleasuring

The temple of my busy dome

Purposely, gently and immensely

Fondling this man's moral ground

For this...mental montage of her inside my head

Mitigates to no end as for her

No matter the situation as I continue to remain calm

Replaying the erotic thoughts of yesteryear

When all I did was trace my tongue

Over every millimeter of Ms. Mystic's favorite

Strawberry mango, flavorlicious essential lip balm

It's these, those mellow recollections of perfection

I worship and will continue to pray upon

Moments like these that I will forever hold dear and

I will never ever, ever let go of because

Our love like a testament of time

Its...paramount

It will forever remain strong...everlasting and serene

For she is my one and only grand, sensual, habitual

Every touch you couldn't comprehend

Every stroke you wouldn't know what I mean

Because I could die tonight 5000 times over

Only to wake up out of my slumber my

Last forty winks wishing to tell her of my

Last 5000 visions and predictions and

Every one of my...last Kodak moment dream's

As if all my predictions and premonitions had

All stood up at once, shouted kicked and screamed

Every divine symbolic analogy

Of her birth given celebrity

Paramour...I love you

Please don't let our bond rest in vein

Please don't let our bond be

Left

Un-remedied.

SPARE CHANGE
====

Some say...absence makes

The heart grow fonder and by

Having someone walk out of your life then

Find their way back again is an act that should

Be held with great gratitude

An action considered to be honored

For she must truly be my...forever flower

Mi amour...something truly meant to be

But if that was the case and

If I ever meant anything

To her from day one...I mean...our beginning

How could she even begin to fix her body

In a position of action that would have her

Pick up all of our shared moments and memories

Extend that right leg and

Extend that right arm

Reach for that door knob...twist turn and leave and

In turn...leaving me sick and overwhelmed while

Self consumed frozen in a state of...disbelief?

So as I now wallow in this new found pain

Fumbling through life tripping over loneliness

I've fallen into this pool overflowing with

Self pity, distain and grief

Will I survive?

One of the many thoughts

That comes to mind as

I descend helplessly deeper into an abyss of

Shit...my world of blame and guilt

Rewinding and replaying...our memories of

Holding hands and slowly k i s s i n g

While standing as if we were two sand

Sculptures purposely created on a naked beach

But sadly...as fate would have it

Never totally out of reach of the ever rising tide

Yet even still, at times

I would often reach out to her yet never find

Calling her name from out the other room while

Failing to realize...she's gone...she's...out of my life

So what to do now with my...long empty days

Hot as fire and my numbing

Freezing cold lonely nights?

I guess I could re-read the poems I've

Already written her for the millionth time or

Compile a million more visual sights

With the material she's just given me and

Put it all on paper cry again and

Try my best not to commit suicide or

Maybe I should just re-focus and try

To make another CD of all our favorite songs

You know...all of our favorite ones we swore

Were only meant for her and me

Like...Best Friends by Tweet

It's...Getting Late by Floetry and

Jill Scott's classic...Honey Molasses...ebony majestry

Damn them joints was magic and

Now whenever I hear um I can't help

But reminisce and imagine all the times

I touched that body while I now touch myself and

Remember every word so cherry sweet

That she would...whisper in my ear and ultimately

Calm my nerves and softly rock me to sleep

Can you imagine me a man so grown yet so sad and broken

My...future predicted by me

Loneliness is the forecast while

Times are so dismal

A life without her is so bleak

I fail at life without her but it aint like she cares

Cause if she had any eyes for me she would see

That my love for her has remained strong

No matter what she's done to me

No matter what she said and especially

No matter how far she's run along

She...turned my world inside out

By telling me we were finished just days after

Telling me...with me is only where she

Needs to be and belongs

Now look at me....all I have left of what we shared

Is the spare change in my front pocket from

My shattered heart...our broken love....

# SPLIT PERSONALITY

Melancholy and relief

The duality of...emotions

As I welcome the new year

A new month, a new day and

A new radio yet

It's playing the same old damn song

Fuck...how long has it been?

Grew my hair out cut it off

Grew it back again and in the interim

I find I...still can't move on

So much for closure

So much for continuing on

While I keep having these...infallible visions of

Magnificence that continue to grip and...prolong

Teasing me with bright flashes of

That hot caramel round

Throwin it back like we got 10 seconds left and

It's 4th and beyond long

But this game of her in my head never rests

Cause she's always on stage hypnotizing me

Poppin that...cherry red thong

Oh the misery of the memories

Oh how they continue to haunt

Memories of a past life

Do I hold on or loose as...confusion ensues

Shit...God knows I was dead ass wrong

Sippin on somethin bubbly while

Gettin bubbly with an imitation blond

Gone off the grid, we both in a back room hiding and

I'm...pulling back that...coarse and peroxide blond

Flickering a snake like tongue till

That clit was pulsating and animated

She was...glistening and strong

You see I've...somehow lost my identity

As my personality is split and

Like David Banner I...transform

Look at me goin all in with octopus palms

As I whisper to myself

May God have mercy on my soul as

I pull that ass to the edge of the bed and

Pull to the side that cherry red thong

Wreakin them pretty cream sheets and

Fuckin up them down filled pillows

Cause that stroke was deadly and

That session was steamy and damn long

While...together we churn and calorie burn

To the tune of our own song

With no concern for those affiliated

No concern for the laws of nature

Like the gravitational pull of the

Earth rotating around the Sun and

The only concern that mattered that night

Was lights camera and action, these

Selfish acts of timeless satisfaction

That all added up to a swollen bag of babies

While she was riding me off into the sunset

On the edge of a burgundy velvet chase lounge

Then helplessly collapsing into my bosom and

Feeling no pressure at all to exchange names or

Numbers as...this was only lust for the moment

A unified effort in elation

A joint effort exercise into an explicit

Minute of...physical attraction!

# SWEET DREAMS

My sugar coated, candied lemon drop

So rich and delectable she

Homemade, sticky, soft and

I love the way she kisses my lips, my body

She's so...methodical in her maneuvers

That once she begins

The combined heat causes us to

Melt like...butterscotch and

The only other thought

That occupies my mind thereafter is

Her on bottom and...me on top

I'd do it anywhere she pleases shit

I swear I'd mail out the invitations

To this inaugural event

Hell we can let the whole world watch

Me and my...one and only luscious succulent

Ms...hot chocolate brown

As I franticly try to find the words

That best describe the lust

Flipping through all appropriate

Adjectives, verbs and nouns

Until the sound of her in thought echoes invariably

In between my cranium eternally and for that

She receives my...forever applauds

I mean...just the mere thought of

Her alone excites me to the point

That I become instantaneously aroused

I mean...just look at her...she so addictive

She's my drug, my vice, my loud and

Right now she got me lifted like levitation and

With each and every thought

She leaves me with

Red eyes and a...cotton mouth

I be...so, so lost without her in my world

But when we get back together look at me

She got my head floating

My brain is stuck way, way up in the clouds

Craving to be her continuously anointed

Her universally blessed and

Within her essence so, so forever doused

For...she is the key maker to the gates of our future

My home that she so perfectly...makes a house!

# TEAZ

She love me

Only two days a week

Not enough room in her heart

For a full set of seven so

She keep me in the dark and

Lead me along like

She got a carrot on a string

Sexy but fake

The only thing stopping me

From wanting to be a starter on her team

Cause believe me when I say that

I've...had the visions and I've lived the dreams

Know...nowhere this is headed but

Play the game whenever she wishes

Cause for her, I be her one and only sole beneficiary and

As such...daily from thee I graciously receive

Any and all of her mitigated

Crumbs on the table mere scraps if anything

Nothing ever of substance for the offering yet

She remains an open book

Full on conversation the only sacrifice as

Her girlfriend she strangely refers to me?

All thanks but no thanks because

I'm a full grown Man

Has she not witnessed

The rings around my roots and all

The branches hanging from my girthy tree?

Is she not...aware of the shade

My body can create as I manifest

These visions of her legs wide spread

Whilst laying down under me?

Purposely insane she's attempting to drive me

Envisioning dreams in repetition

The texture of lace panties...the color of coffee cream

Resting upon...skin I imagine to be as

Soft as silk

Giving off the reflection of a caramel sheen

Leaving me to wake up to silly fantasies

These silly dreams

Head doctor only wants attention for

The duration of a train ride

Her...muse she's attempting to make of me

Yet I remain well aware of all the self inflicted contradiction

Yet I remain not strong enough to walk away and

Not strong enough to set sail and from her bullshit...flee

These downtown dirty, stank, piss infested streets

Leading me down dimly lit blue line isles

Where...she can sit against the window and

Whisper her most intimate nighttime themes of

Her not out of the shower

Yet spiritually she's dripping all over me

While...I'm outside looking in and my surrogate

Is acting out our fantasy, buzzing through the evening

Sailing her delicate seven seas, that...vibrator

She purchased, prayed to and

Ceremoniously named after me

She's got me...listening to every word

While I'm pitching a tent wishing

She'd...stop with this elaborate

Dalliance this...sophisticated

Senseless nickel and dance tease

Why is she...in my head and...fucking with me?

Why can't this...tension she ease and

Begin to quill this pain?

Shit!

I need her lips up against me and mine while

Together we create heavy thoughts

That are sure to forever remain engraved in our brains

Shit...I can see it in her eyes

I know she gotta feels the same it's

The way she smiles when I come around

Shy for no reason yet she has

Complete masturbation sessions she confessed that

She ritualistically dedicates to me and are

All in the honor my name

SHIT...

For once can't you just stop being a teaz and

Let me taste that pussy, I wanna smell it, feel it

FUCK....

Let's stop playing this

Sadistic game!

# THE DIALOG

We both play deaf and appear to act...tongue-tied

We've...lost all of our unity in our spirituality and

Now we're merely only inclined

To ritualistically throw up

Gangland hand signs while

Speaking in an ancient dialect that

Even we don't recognize...and

I can only think that we could possibly be better off

Using a dance or maybe even a simple pantomime

To show a crowd of strangers how you've...mentally

Checked out and...no longer desire to be mine

All because on my phone all I can seem to find are

Broken sentences...mean memes and

Countless hours of...dead time

Nothing but silence since

Everything about us has become so...Anti

So...whatever happened to my Shorty?

Whatever happened to my...sunshine?

She got me...mulling around here in the darkness

Stumbling over memories living out

Scripted scenes from a memoir of her past lies

Exasperated from feeling like this shit here

This shit right here...I don't want and...I don't like

Hell, we can't even sit down so we can share a cup of act right

Cause we're always so...uptight and

It seems as though love was only infatuation as

Emotions have mysteriously crashed just

Shortly after taking flight

It used to feel like

Everything with her was so right until shit just went...so left

I spilled the contents of my heart

Thinking that it actually meant something but

In the end I only ended up with an empty chest

As I blame it all on this day and age

Where we can't even have a conversation

Fuck all this...dumb ass high tech

You see...somehow we got...lost in translation and

Can't even communicate cause we're too busy

Fumbling over emotions and emojis

All lost within a fractured text

Whatever happened to

Looking at someone face to face

Instead of a phone screen to feel that pain

To experience that anguish?

I just needed to see you...was that too much to request?

Well it probably was because

Even though you thought you might be done with me

You also knew further down

That I could possibly fix this mess with

My eyes locked upon your eyes

Ask me how I know you can't resist?

We both...suspended in time

We...inhale as my breath becomes one with your breath as

My...hands gently begin reeling you in and

We can't help but...deep kiss

My...body against your body as

We melt as one together and

Your...flesh beckons to become one with my flesh!

# THE ENERGY WE SHARE

Your energy

I feel it

Reading these words

You are...one with me as

Each letter traces back at your eyes like

I am the screen and at any brightness

Any font you choose

It is me gazing back at she

Changing the narrative

For...this is not just a poem

This is not just a story

This is me reaching out touching you through

An extraterrestrial spiritual

Channeled dimension

So just...slow your heart beat

Read me slower

Can't you hear my voice?

Shhhh...listen?

Fall...deeper into my soul and

I promise to catch you

While unbeknownst to you you've already

Wholeheartedly

In love and in lust already fallen

I speak directly to you

Because these words were created for you

Taylor made for you

Do you not remember you've...already told me

Exactly what it is you wanted?

Someone who listens

Someone who cares

Someone who tells you they miss

You during the day and

Someone who will fuck you like

A stranger in the night then

Hold you when it's all over and

When it's all said and done

This love...don't ever question

How did he know?

When it was I who was...put here for you because

For centuries this has been in the books as

Our story has already been...written

Meant to be as if

You are my Earth and I am your Sun

Our...energy is gravitational

While my words are our Galaxy

We were meant to be and...we will always be...one!

# TRUST

My dearest, my love

Have I ever told you

That from day one it's been you I want?

That thousand yard stare from

Across a crowded room

That energy from we couldn't run

Electrified the melanin

Out in the dead of night feeling

Like I just been grazed by

The rays of the Lord's most white hot Sun

For how blessed is he?

Dizziness is the outcome

It was like staring down the double barrel

Of a flame throwing shotgun while

Punch drunk off Jamaican rum

Craving to be that...last one

That...last dream, that last wish

That... last twirling tongue

As I celebrate the grandeur of our union

The only way I know how

Buck, buck, buck to the seventh power

I salute you...21 gun

As we toast with the sweetest wine...plum and

Pray that this bond will forever remain strong and

Last night after night while our

Hallways remain littered with rose pedals and

Our rooms always be filled by

Iridescent candle light

While...soft melodies reign over midnight airways and

Trigger that...nostalgic insight

As...we perform ritualistically over one another

Every day and every night until the...break of dawn

Until we together work up enough sweat and

In the end in unison collapse...pant and bite

Leaving me with this only thought of you

Forever remaining mine and

With me you..spending the rest of your life...

# VIOLET HUES

Elicit these

Violet hues

Sadistic these

Tantric dreams I

Nightly have of you

She leaves my reality...virtual she

8K, 3D, HD

Ass and hips widescreen

Got me feenin, feelin like I can

Reach right out and touch you

Suck on you

Meanwhile the visual of

Pink slits and ring clits poking through

Those Vicky Secrets in plain view

Leaving my issue a situation considered critical

From miraculous wet spots that

Soak religiously from rising sea levels and

Eventually trickle down way below

While we grinding methodically

While we kissing slow and

I got two fingers delicately tracing lace

As I stare in her face and palm the middle

That...soft, soft and that damp, damp as

She say to me sweetie, insert um both

While...she zoning in and out and

Aaliyah we listening to...and

It's ironic...because at the same time I was

Trying to rock the boat, rock the boat

Trying to act out a scene of a Trey Songz video because

I swear that body I just wanted to drive into...splash

All because of the way she governs and rules my life

She leaves me no choice but to

Label her my permanent pastime paradise because

Sex with her I swear is just like

Source magazine's 5 mic's

The way she...bum rush the stage and

Flow on dat mic she

Rockin that crown while

My eyes roll back and my spirit take flight

So I...push down on her crown and

Mumble to her softly

Bitch It's a cold, cold life while

The furthest notion from my mind

Was whether or not this was

Wrong or right because

I dwell in a home of sin and pain and

It ain't in me to chastise

Especially when she's giving me that

Face Time all the way live and

I give her a look that's so, so mesmerized

I mean...just look at the size of them

Big ass bubbles that pop while she was

Lookin like she was blowin on a big ass blow pop

Having me envisioning explosions creamier and louder

Than that of a Champaign bottle

Once it's shook and the cork pops off

While...tipsy I remain from the way

She spit that fire so masterful

As that sloppy was way off the top

While she's...hands free, Bluetooth

You should see the way she

Spit it out, don't let go

Look me dead in the eye

Then slurp that shit back up

Fuck she's...nasty the way she lives in my thoughts

Always keeping me with a grimace on my face

Like two girls and a fuckin cup

While my...entire world and mental capacity

Because of her shall eternally remain corrupt

I'm...intoxicated off them pink hues

That...leave me confused

As my emotions continuously run amuck....

# WILD EMBERS

Like a Forrest fire out of control

She tore through my existence

She...blew into my world like

Wild embers

Rapidly consuming my soul

Disrupting the dichotomy

Setting ablaze my fiber

Deconstructing me inch by inch and

Inevitably...became that

Mystifying flame I could never bear to extinguish

She had me...weak at the knees

Because I had lacked any respectable

Preventive measures as

Resistance levels was at an all-time low

While it all started from the thought of our

Very...first...kiss

Her lips, those lips...an...oasis

For a thirsty man lost for a millennium

Lost in the barren wilderness

With a heart full of desire and

No one in his life worthy enough

For him to bestow upon and truly bless

Until her wild embers

Until her forest fire

Until her ravenous lips....

www.ingramcontent.com/pod-product-compliance
Lightning Source LLC
LaVergne TN
LVHW041321080426
835513LV00008B/543